Jo's Little Favorites

Timeless Quilts from Scraps and Fat Quarters

JO MORTON

Jo's Little Favorites:
Timeless Quilts from Scraps and Fat Quarters
© 2016 by Jo Morton

Martingale®
19021 120th Ave. NE, Ste. 102
Bothell, WA 98011-9511 USA
ShopMartingale.com

Printed in China
21 20 19 18 17 16   8 7 6 5 4 3 2

**Library of Congress Cataloging-in-Publication Data
is available upon request.**

ISBN: 978-1-60468-739-2

Mission Statement
Dedicated to providing quality products
and service to inspire creativity.

Credits

PUBLISHER AND CHIEF VISIONARY OFFICER
Jennifer Erbe Keltner

EDITORIAL DIRECTOR
Karen Costello Soltys

DESIGN DIRECTOR
Paula Schlosser

MANAGING EDITOR
Tina Cook

PRODUCTION MANAGER
Regina Girard

ACQUISITIONS EDITOR
Karen M. Burns

STUDIO PHOTOGRAPHY
Brent Kane

TECHNICAL EDITOR
Mary Helen Schiltz

LOCATION PHOTOGRAPHY
Adam Albright

COPY EDITOR
Marcy Heffernan

ILLUSTRATOR
Christine Erikson

SPECIAL THANKS
To the staff of The Garden Barn of Indianola, Iowa,
thank you for generously allowing us to take
photographs on location. For more information,
visit www.TheGardenBarn.com

Contents

Introduction

I began my quiltmaking journey in 1980, taking a 14-week class in Lincoln, Nebraska. And quite a journey it was—50 miles each way—to learn to make quilts. In that class we made 14" blocks for a double-bed quilt in the quilt-as-you-go method that was popular at the time. We pieced by hand, cut templates by hand, and quilted by hand. That may sound like a lot of work in today's rotary-cutting, chain-piecing world. But I was hooked.

When it came to quiltmaking, I wanted to learn everything I could. But it wasn't until 1985 that I discovered my true love. That's when I made my first quilt that looked old. It was a four-block quilt made with 6" Cake Stand blocks. I hand quilted it to death! That's also when I realized that to make all the quilts that inspired me, I needed to make small quilts, not bed-sized ones. Otherwise, I'd never be able to finish them all. Besides, we have a small 1920s bungalow home with no large wall spaces to display big quilts. And sharing a home with kitties meant at least one would always be sleeping on a quilt if it were on a bed.

Don't get me wrong; I've made a few bed-sized quilts over the years. But I'm really drawn to small quilts made to look old by using reproduction fabrics and traditional blocks of the era. They make perfect class projects. Not every quilt needs to be a long-term project!

And all of this led to two of my favorite projects over the years—designing reproduction fabrics for quilters and designing small quilts for my Jo's Little Women Club, which is now in its 13th year. The quilts in this book were originally designed as part of one club year or another, but here you'll find I've curated a selection of favorite quilts from over the years. Some have been remade in newer reproduction fabrics, and some appear just as they were. I love how the reproduction prints from over the years can blend and work together, making it easy to combine prints from your stash with the latest collections at your local quilt shop.

I'll always make small quilts, as I enjoy displaying and seeing them in various places in our home. They're fun to make, possible to complete in a relatively short time, and they offer countless ways to decorate your home. Just as you can see in the beautiful photographs in this book, you too can enjoy small quilts tucked into a wide variety of spaces. So enjoy the process, make one or all 13, and have fun showing off these little quilts in unexpected areas of your home.

Stack small quilts on the seats of child-sized chairs for a pint-sized display.

Materials

Yardage is based on 42"-wide fabric. Fat quarters are 18" x 21".

½ yard *total* of assorted green prints for Log Cabin blocks

1 fat quarter of holly print for center square of Log Cabin blocks

4 fat quarters *each* of assorted gold prints and assorted red prints for logs

1 fat quarter *OR* ¼ yard of tan print for single-fold binding

⅝ yard of fabric for backing

23" x 29" piece of batting

Cutting

All of the logs and border strips are cut from the lengthwise grain (parallel to the selvages), so that the blocks will lie flat. Crosswise strips have more stretch, making it more difficult to keep the blocks flat and smooth. If you fold the fabric to cut it, take care that the strips stay straight as you cut them. You may have to trim the cut edge of the fabric from time to time to straighten it, and then cut more strips.

The number of strips you need for each gold and red print depends on where the strips are placed in the block and how often the print is repeated. Start by cutting four strips of each print, and then cut more as needed.

From the holly-print fat quarter, cut:
12 squares, 2½" x 2½"

From the *lengthwise* grain of the assorted green prints, cut:
30 or more strips, at least 1" x 18" or longer

From the *lengthwise* grain of *each* gold print, cut:
4 strips, 1" x 18"

From the *lengthwise* grain of *each* red print, cut:
4 strips, 1" x 18"

From the *crosswise* grain of the tan print, cut:
6 strips, 1⅛" x 21", for binding

If you're like me and have a love of antiques and old treasures, consider this idea. An old window frame can act as a "frame" for any small quilt. Hang the quilt on the wall beneath the frame, and your eye fills in the pattern behind the muntins. Swap out quilts by season, change a few accessories, and you've got a simple display for small quilts year 'round.

FINISHED QUILT: 18½" x 24½" ✂ FINISHED BLOCK: 6" x 6"

Jo's Little Favorites

Making the Blocks

1. Follow the numbered strips in the block diagram and the sequence of colors below to make each Log Cabin block. Place each strip under the square or unit when sewing them together. It's important to use an accurate ¼"-wide seam allowance to make the blocks finish the same size.

Round 1:
gold print #1 for positions 1 and 2;
green print #1 for positions 3 and 4

Round 2:
red print #1 for positions 5 and 6;
green print #2 for positions 7 and 8

Round 3:
gold print #2 for positions 9 and 10;
green print #3 for positions 11 and 12

Round 4:
red print #2 for positions 13 and 14;
green print #4 for positions 15 and 16

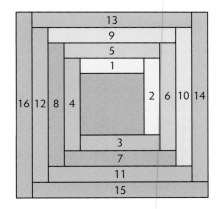

2. Sew a holly-print 2½" square to the gold #1 strip, right sides together. Press the seam allowances away from the square. Using a rotary cutter and mat and an acrylic ruler, trim the gold strip ends even with the square.

3. Sew a second gold #1 strip right sides together to the right edge of the unit. Press the seam allowances away from the square. Trim the gold strip ends even with the unit.

4. Sew a green #1 strip right sides together to the bottom edge of the unit. Press the seam allowances away from the square. Trim the green strip ends even with the unit.

5. Sew a second green #1 strip right sides together to the left edge of the unit. Press the seam allowances away from the square. Trim the green strip ends even with the unit. You have now added log-cabin strips to four sides of the center square, completing round 1. Square the unit to 3½" x 3½".

6. Sew, trim, and press as before to add four more strips in clockwise rotation around the unit—two strips of red #1 and two strips of green #2. Square the unit to 4½" x 4½".

7. Continue to sew, trim, and press as before to add four more strips in clockwise rotation around the unit—two strips of gold #2 and two strips of green #3. Square the unit to 5½" x 5½".

8. Continue to sew, trim, and press as before to add four more strips in clockwise rotation around the unit—two strips of red #2 and two strips of green #4. Square the unit to 6½" x 6½" to make a Log Cabin block.

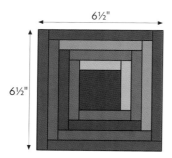

9. Repeat steps 2–8 to make a total of 12 Log Cabin blocks.

Assembling the Quilt Top

1. Arrange the Log Cabin blocks in four rows of three blocks each, rotating each block so the green prints are in the lower-left corner.

2. Sew the blocks in each row together. Press the seam allowances open.

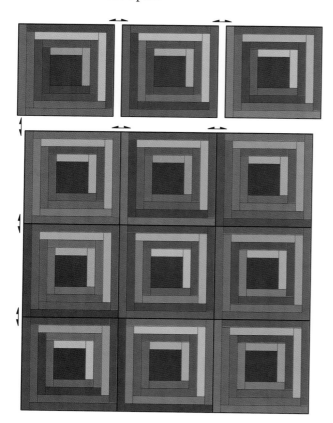

Quilt assembly

3. Pin the rows together, matching the seam intersections. Sew the rows together. Press the seam allowances open.

For a flatter finished quilt and easier quilting, press the seam allowances open when joining rows.

Finishing the Quilt

For more detailed information about any finishing steps, visit ShopMartingale.com/HowtoQuilt.

1. Layer the quilt top, batting, and backing. Baste the layers together.

2. Hand or machine quilt as desired. The quilt shown was machine quilted with an allover Baptist fan pattern. The curved quilting motif makes a nice counterpoint to all the straight logs in the patchwork.

3. Use the tan 1⅛"-wide strips to make and attach single-fold binding. For more detailed information on my technique for making and attaching the binding, see "Single-Fold Binding" on page 78.

4. Make and attach a hanging sleeve, if desired.

5. Make, sign, and date a label and attach it to your quilt.

I never worry about putting my quilts away "for good." I love the idea of using them in everyday life, even putting a plate of cookies atop my quilt—a feast for sweet lovers and fabric lovers alike.

If your little quilt doesn't fit into the bottom of a tray exactly, all is not lost. Simply turn it sideways, even a bit off-kilter, letting it drape over the edges.

Materials

Yardage is based on 42"-wide fabric. Fat quarters are 18" x 21". Fat eighths are 9" x 21".

½ yard *total* of assorted dark prints (pinks and browns) for blocks and sawtooth border

½ yard *total* of assorted light prints (tans and creams) for blocks and sawtooth border

1 fat quarter of brown stripe for sashing

1 fat eighth of dark-pink solid for sashing squares

1 fat eighth of brown plaid for border cornerstones and sawtooth border

1 fat quarter OR ¼ yard of tan print for single-fold binding

⅔ yard of fabric for backing

23" x 23" piece of batting

Cutting

From the assorted dark prints, cut:
45 squares, 1¾" x 1¾"
5 squares, 5" x 5"

From the assorted light prints, cut:
36 squares, 1¾" x 1¾"
5 squares, 5" x 5"

From the brown stripe, cut:
24 strips, 1½" x 4¼"

From the dark-pink solid, cut:
16 squares, 1½" x 1½"

From the brown plaid, cut:
4 squares, 2" x 2"

From the *crosswise* grain of the tan print, cut:
5 strips, 1⅛" x 21", for binding

Making the Blocks

1. Arrange five assorted dark and four assorted light 1¾" squares in three rows of three squares

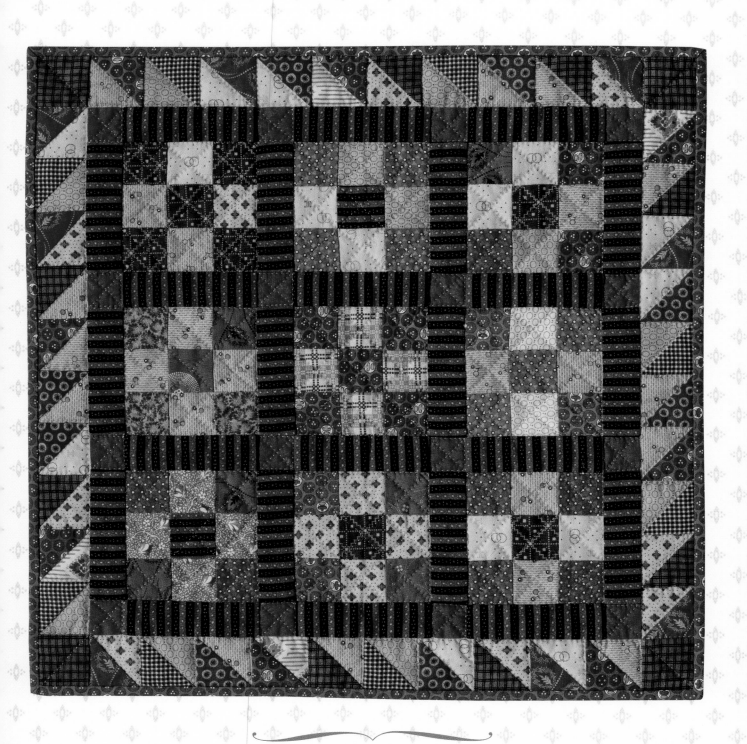

FINISHED QUILT: 18¾" x 18¾" ✂ FINISHED BLOCK: 3¾" x 3¾"

each. Be sure you have a high contrast among your darks and lights so you can distinguish the Nine Patch pattern.

2. Sew the squares in each row together. Press the seam allowances toward the dark squares.

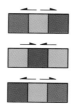

3. Sew the rows together, matching the seam intersections, to make a Nine Patch block. Press the seam allowances open.

You can also press the seam allowances using my "Clipping Trick" on page 78 so the blocks will lie flat without too much bulk at the seam intersections. Press the center squares toward the center and the corner squares toward the corners.

Assembling the Quilt Top

1. Lay out the Nine Patch blocks, brown-striped sashing strips, and dark-pink squares in seven rows.

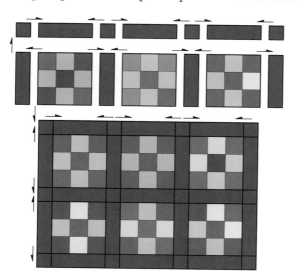

2. Join the pieces to make four sashing rows and three block rows. Press the seam allowances toward the sashing strips.

3. Join the rows, matching the seam intersections. Referring to "Clipping Trick" at seam intersections, press the seam allowances toward the sashing rows.

4. For the sawtooth border, use the light and dark 5" squares and my shortcut technique in "Half-Square-Triangle Trick" on page 15 to make a total of 40 half-square-triangle units.

5. Lay out 10 half-square-triangle units along each side of the quilt top. Rotate each unit so the light-print edges align along the inside edge. Note the direction the triangles are pointing, too.

6. Join the units to make four sawtooth borders using a scant ¼" seam allowance, so each strip measures 15¾" long. (Note that you may have to release a seam or two to make this measurement, since the math comes out to 15" square plus the ½" seam allowance. I find it is easier to take in or let out a couple seams rather than deal with small fractions.) Press the seam allowances toward the dark triangles.

Make 4.

7. Pin and sew two sawtooth borders to opposite sides of the quilt top, with the light triangles toward the quilt center. Press the seam allowances toward the quilt center.

8. Sew the brown-plaid 2" squares to the ends of the remaining two sawtooth borders. Press the seam allowances toward the squares.

9. Pin and sew the borders from step 8 to the remaining sides. Press the seam allowances toward the center. Referring to "Clipping Trick,"

press the seam allowances of the 2" squares toward the corners.

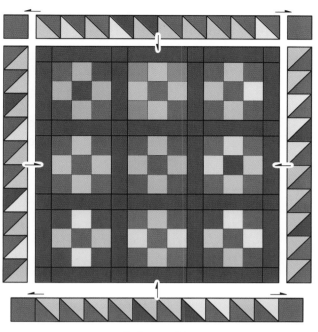

Quilt assembly

Finishing the Quilt

For more detailed information about any finishing steps, visit ShopMartingale.com/HowtoQuilt.

1. Layer the quilt top, batting, and backing. Baste the layers together.

2. Hand or machine quilt as desired. I hand quilted diagonal lines in both directions to create a crosshatch grid, or Xs, through the Nine Patch blocks and sashing squares. I stitched in the ditch along the sashing strips and around each half-square-triangle unit in the border.

3. Use the tan 1⅛"-wide strips to make and attach single-fold binding. For more detailed information on my technique for making and attaching the binding, see "Single-Fold Binding" on page 78.

4. Make and attach a hanging sleeve, if desired.

5. Make, sign, and date a label and attach it to your quilt.

HALF-SQUARE-TRIANGLE TRICK

1. Cut the five light 5" squares in half to make a total of 10 rectangles, 2½" x 5".

2. Place two different light rectangles right sides together on a dark 5" square; press.

3. Draw two diagonal lines, or an X, on the wrong side of the light rectangles. Sew a scant ¼" from each side of the drawn lines.

4. Cut the layered unit in half horizontally and vertically (rectangle edge) first, using your ruler to measure 2½" from each edge. Without moving any of the pieces, cut the units apart on the diagonal pencil lines to make a total of eight half-square-triangle units. Press the seam allowances toward the dark triangle.

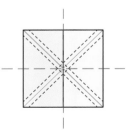

5. Trim each half-square-triangle unit to measure 2" square.

Materials

Yardage is based on 42"-wide fabric. Fat quarters are 18" x 21".

¼ yard of cream print for block backgrounds
⅛ yard of blue print for block star points
1 fat quarter of tan print for setting squares, setting triangles, and corner triangles
1 fat quarter of brown leaf print for border
1 fat quarter of dark-brown print for border cornerstones
1 fat quarter *OR* ¼ yard of dark-orange print for single-fold binding
⅝ yard of fabric for backing
23" x 23" piece of batting

Cutting

The borders are cut from the lengthwise grain (parallel to the selvages); strips cut crosswise have more stretch.

From the blue print, cut:
36 squares, 1⅝" x 1⅝"

From the cream print, cut:
9 squares, 2" x 2"
36 squares, 1¼" x 1¼"
9 squares, 2¾" x 2¾"

From the tan print, cut:
4 squares, 3½" x 3½"
2 squares, 5¾" x 5¾"; cut each square into quarters diagonally to yield 8 setting triangles
2 squares, 3¼" x 3¼"; cut each square in half diagonally to yield 4 corner triangles

From the *lengthwise* grain of the brown leaf print, cut:
4 strips, 3¼" x 13¼"

From the dark-brown print, cut:
4 squares, 3¼" x 3¼"

From the *crosswise* grain of the dark-orange print, cut:
5 strips, 1⅛" x 21", for binding

When using small quilts to decorate throughout your home, consider ways to incorporate them dimensionally, beyond flat on a table or hanging on a wall. It may take a little finessing, but tucking a small quilt into a cupboard adds a pop of color and softness to an otherwise hard surface. Here, a quilt helps a light antique bowl stand out against the cupboard's cream interior—showing off both your treasures and your quilt at once!

FINISHED QUILT: 18¾" x 18¾" ✂ FINISHED BLOCK: 3" x 3"

Making the Blocks

1. Draw a diagonal line from corner to corner on the wrong side of the blue 1⅝" squares.

2. Align two marked squares on opposite corners of a cream 2¾" square, right sides together. Note the squares will overlap in the center. Sew a scant ¼" from each side of the drawn lines.

3. Cut apart on the drawn lines. Press the seam allowances toward the small triangles.

4. Align one blue 1⅝" square on the corner of the large triangle. Note the orientation of the diagonal line. Sew a scant ¼" from each side of the drawn line. Cut apart on the drawn line. Press the seam allowances toward the blue triangles to make a flying-geese unit. Repeat with the remaining pieces to make a total of four flying-geese units. Square these units to measure 1¼" x 2".

  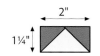

5. Lay out the cream 2" square and 1¼" squares and the flying-geese units in three rows. Sew the squares and units into rows. Press the seam allowances toward the squares.

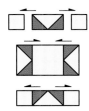

6. Pin and sew the rows together, matching seam intersections, to make a Sawtooth Star block. Press the seam allowances toward the middle row.

7. Refer to "Clipping Trick" on page 78 to clip the four seam intersections. Press the flying-geese units toward the center, press the squares toward the corners, and press the seam intersections open. The Sawtooth Star block should measure 3½" x 3½". Trim as needed.

8. Repeat steps 2–7 to make a total of nine Sawtooth Star blocks.

Assembling the Quilt Top

1. Lay out the Sawtooth Star blocks with the tan setting squares and setting triangles in five diagonal rows.

2. Sew the pieces in each row together. Press the seam allowances toward the setting pieces.

3. Pin and sew the rows together, matching seam intersections. Refer to "Clipping Trick" at the seam intersections. Press the seam allowances toward the setting pieces. Press the clipped intersections open.

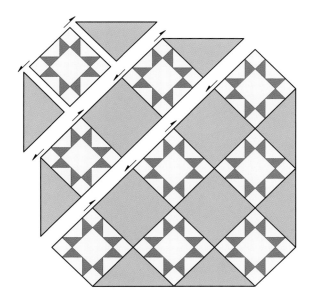

4. Add the tan corner triangles; press the seam allowances toward the corner triangles. Trim the setting triangles and corner triangles (they were cut slightly oversize), making sure to leave a ¼" seam allowance beyond the points. Square the quilt top to measure 13¼" x 13¼".

5. Sew two brown-leaf 3¼" x 13¼" strips to opposite sides of the quilt top. Press the seam allowances toward the border.

6. Sew the dark-brown 3¼" squares to the ends of the remaining brown-leaf 3¼" x 13¼" strips. Press the seam allowances toward the strips.

7. Pin and sew the borders, matching seam intersections, to the top and bottom of the quilt top. Press the seam allowances toward the border. Referring to "Clipping Trick," press the seam allowances of the squares toward the corners; press the seam intersections open.

Finishing the Quilt

For more detailed information about any finishing steps, visit ShopMartingale.com/HowtoQuilt.

1. Layer the quilt top, batting, and backing. Baste the layers together.

2. Hand or machine quilt as desired. I hand quilted in the ditch around all the star points of each block and around each block and the border. Then I stitched horizontal and vertical lines through each block, and echoed these stitches in the setting squares. Diagonal lines in the setting squares echo the flying-geese angles in the blocks, creating chevron designs. Parallel diagonal lines accent the setting triangles and border.

3. Use the dark-orange 1⅛"-wide strips to make and attach single-fold binding. For more detailed information on my technique for making and attaching the binding, see "Single-Fold Binding" on page 78.

4. Make and attach a hanging sleeve, if desired.

5. Make, sign, and date a label and attach it to your quilt.

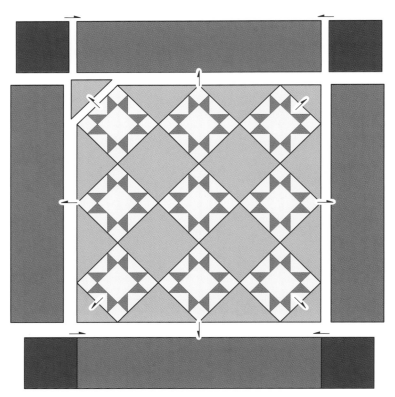

Quilt assembly

Double X

Even when they're not the "stars" of the season, little quilts can play a supporting roll in your decorating.

As you hang your favorite quilt during the holidays, don't put away the other small quilts for the season. Instead, roll each into a tube and tuck them into a basket. If you have trouble getting them to stand, roll a small piece of batting inside for extra support.

Materials

Yardage is based on 42"-wide fabric. Fat eighths are 9" x 21".

25 fat eighths or scraps of assorted light prints for blocks
25 fat eighths or scraps of assorted dark (red, green, and brown) prints for blocks and sashing squares
½ yard of tan print for sashing strips
½ yard of green stripe for sashing squares, setting and corner triangles, and border cornerstones
1 yard of red-and-green print for border
1 fat quarter OR ¼ yard of red print for single-fold binding
1¼ yards of fabric for backing
45" x 45" piece of batting

Cutting

The border and sashing strips are cut from the lengthwise grain (parallel to the selvages) as this has the least stretch or give in a fabric. That's helpful in piecing your quilt accurately and results in a nice, flat quilt top. Strips cut crosswise have more stretch.

From *each* assorted light print, cut:
3 squares, 2½" x 2½" (75 total)

From *each* assorted dark print, cut:
3 squares, 2" x 2" (75 total)
3 squares, 2½" x 2½" (75 total)

From the remaining assorted red prints, cut:
16 squares, 1½" x 1½"

From the *lengthwise* grain of the tan print, cut:
64 strips, 1½" x 5"

From the green stripe, cut:
3 squares, 7¾" x 7¾"; cut each square into quarters diagonally to yield 12 setting triangles
2 squares, 6" x 6"; cut each square in half diagonally to yield 4 corner triangles
4 squares, 5" x 5"
24 squares, 1½" x 1½"

Continued on page 24

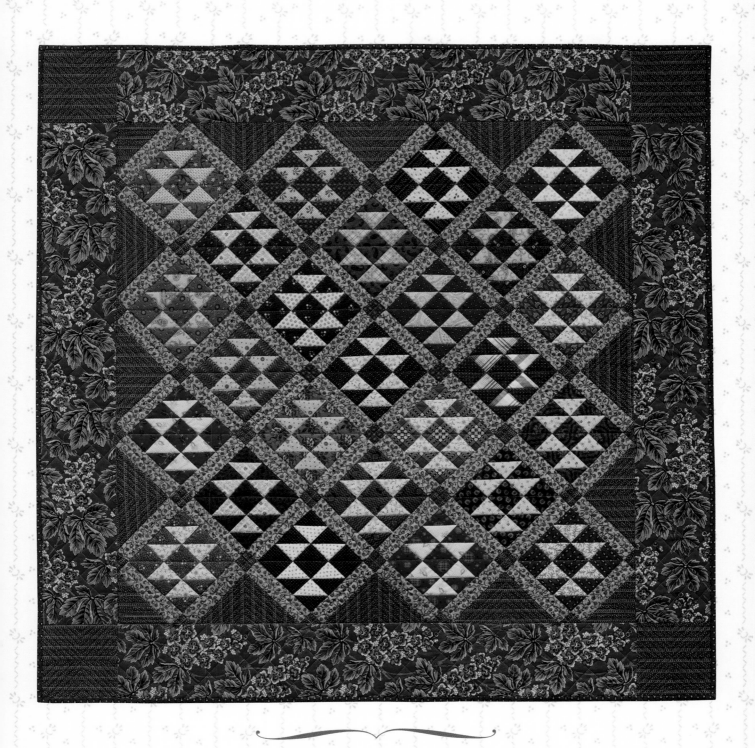

FINISHED QUILT: 40¼" x 40¼" ✂ FINISHED BLOCK: 4½" x 4½"

Continued from page 22

From the *lengthwise* grain of the red-and-green print, cut:
4 strips, 5" x 31¾"

From the *crosswise* grain of the red print, cut:
9 strips, 1⅛" x 21", for binding

Making the Blocks

1. Draw a diagonal line from corner to corner on the wrong side of three light 2½" squares.

2. Using three matching dark-print squares, lay a marked light square on top of a dark 2½" square, right sides together. Sew a scant ¼" from each side of the drawn line.

3. Cut each unit apart on the drawn line to make six half-square-triangle units. Press the seam allowances toward the dark triangle. Trim the unit to measure 2" x 2".

4. Lay out the half-square-triangle units and three 2" squares that match the dark triangles in three rows, orienting the light triangles as shown.

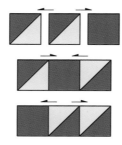

5. Sew the units and squares together in each row. Press the seam allowances toward the corners in the first and third rows and toward the dark square in the middle row.

6. Pin and sew the rows together, matching seam intersections, to make a Double X block. Press the seam allowances toward the first and third rows.

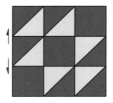

7. Refer to "Clipping Trick" on page 78 for the seam intersections, so the block will lie flat; continue to press the seam allowances toward the darker print.

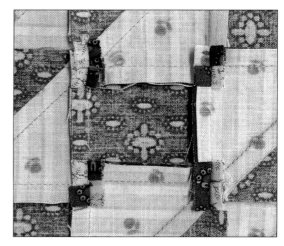

By clipping into the seam allowances, you can press the seams flat.

8. Make a total of 25 Double X blocks. The quilt shown has 11 red, 11 green, and 3 brown blocks.

ACCURACY COUNTS

Basic quiltmaking skills, including using an accurate *scant* ¼" seam allowance and accurate rotary cutting and measuring, are necessary so these smaller-scale quilts will go together nicely.

Assembling the Quilt Top

The blocks, sashing strips, and squares are assembled in diagonal rows. Press all the seam allowances toward the sashing strips and squares. The setting and corner triangles are added at the ends of the rows. They were cut oversized and will be trimmed after the quilt center is assembled.

1. Lay out the Double X blocks, tan sashing strips, assorted red and green-striped sashing squares, and the green-striped setting triangles in 15 diagonal rows. Note that the red sashing squares are all in the center of the quilt. Use the green-striped sashing squares around the outer edge and the next row in, near the corners.

2. Sew the pieces in each row together. Press the seam allowances toward the sashing strips.

3. Pin and sew the rows together, matching seam intersections. Refer to "Clipping Trick" for the seam intersections. Press the seam allowances toward the sashing rows.

4. Add the green-striped corner triangles; press the seam allowances toward the sashing. Trim the setting triangles and corner triangles (they were cut slightly oversize), making sure to leave a ¼" seam allowance beyond the outer intersections of the sashing strips and squares. Square the quilt top to measure 31¾" x 31¾".

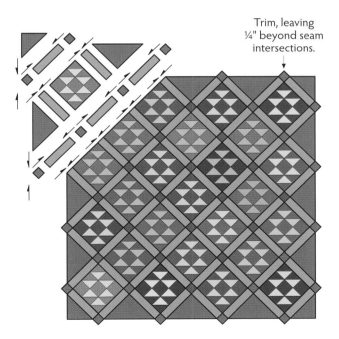

Trim, leaving ¼" beyond seam intersections.

5. Sew two red-and-green 5" x 31¾" strips to opposite sides of the quilt top. Press the seam allowances toward the border.

6. Sew the green-striped 5" squares to the ends of the remaining red-and-green 5" x 31¾" strips. Press the seam allowances toward the strips.

7. Pin and sew the borders, matching seam intersections, to the top and bottom of the quilt. Press the seam allowances toward the border. Using the clipping trick for the seam intersections, press the seam allowances of the squares toward the corners; press the seam intersections open.

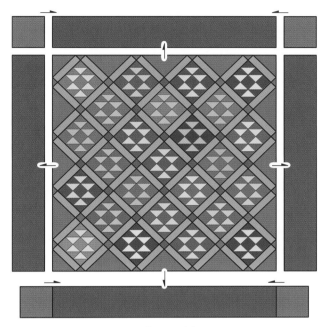

Quilt assembly

Finishing the Quilt

For more detailed information about any finishing steps, visit ShopMartingale.com/HowtoQuilt.

1. Layer the quilt top, batting, and backing. Baste the layers together.

2. Hand or machine quilt as desired. The quilt shown is machine quilted with straight lines through the vertical center of each sashing strip. The blocks are quilted through the horizontal center. The setting triangles are quilted with a series of six peaked lines for emphasis, and the border is quilted with a diagonal crosshatch grid.

3. Use the red 1⅛"-wide strips to make and attach single-fold binding. For more detailed information on my technique for making and attaching the binding, see "Single-Fold Binding" on page 78.

4. Make and attach a hanging sleeve, if desired.

5. Make, sign, and date a label and attach it to your quilt.

Materials

Yardage is based on 42"-wide fabric. Fat quarters are 18" x 21". Fat eighths are 9" x 18".

1 fat quarter of red-and-cream toile print for center square

1 fat eighth *each* of 4 red and 4 cream prints for borders 1–8

⅝ yard of red leaf print for outer border

1 fat quarter OR ¼ yard of tan print for binding

⅝ yard of fabric for backing

23" x 23" piece of batting

FUSSY-CUTTING THE CENTER SQUARE

Center a 7½" square ruler over the fat quarter of red-and-cream toile print, being careful to allow for the seam allowance when centering so that important parts of the design aren't cropped. If you use a larger square ruler, use colored tape to mask off the 7½" square window before centering the ruler over the fabric. Double check before cutting!

Cutting

Cut all border strips from the lengthwise grain (parallel to the selvages) to control the amount of stretch. This will help ensure your quilt is square and true; strips cut crosswise have more stretch.

From the red-and-cream toile print, fussy-cut:
1 square, 7½" x 7½"

From red print #1 (border 1), cut:
2 strips, 1" x 7½"
2 strips, 1" x 8½"

From cream print #1 (border 2), cut:
2 strips, 1" x 8½"
2 strips, 1" x 9½"

The fussy-cut center medallion on this little beauty is perfectly suited to be shown with nothing atop it. However, sometimes you want a little shape and height at the center of your table. In that case, consider a clear vessel for a centerpiece. Choosing something you can see through covers up less of the quilt visually, while still giving your decor the desired scale and size.

Continued on page 29

FINISHED QUILT: 18½" x 18½"

Continued from page 27

From red print #2 (border 3), cut:
2 strips, 1" x 9½"
2 strips, 1" x 10½"

From cream print #2 (border 4), cut:
2 strips, 1" x 10½"
2 strips, 1" x 11½"

From red print #3 (border 5), cut:
2 strips, 1" x 11½"
2 strips, 1" x 12½"

From cream print #3 (border 6), cut:
2 strips, 1" x 12½"
2 strips, 1" x 13½"

From red print #4 (border 7), cut:
2 strips, 1" x 13½"
2 strips, 1" x 14½"

From cream print #4 (border 8), cut:
2 strips, 1" x 14½"
2 strips, 1" x 15½"

From the *lengthwise* grain of the red leaf print, cut:
2 strips, 2" x 15½"
2 strips, 2" x 18½"

From the *crosswise* grain of the tan print, cut:
5 strips, 1⅛" x 21", for binding

Assembling the Quilt Top

Sew the sashing strips around the center square in the Courthouse Steps manner, as described below.

1. Sew the 1" x 7½" red print #1 strips to opposite sides of the red-and-cream toile-print square. Press the seam allowances away from the center.

2. Sew the 1" x 8½" red print #1 strips to the top and bottom of the square. Press the seam allowances away from the center. Your unit should now measure 8½" x 8½".

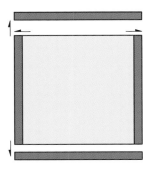

3. Sew the 1" x 8½" cream print #1 strips to opposite sides of the square. Press the seam allowances away from the center.

4. Sew the 1" x 9½" cream print #1 strips to the top and bottom of the square. Press the seam allowances away from the center. Your unit should now measure 9½" x 9½".

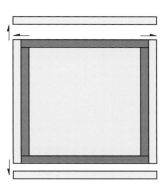

5. Continue to add the border strips in sequence, pressing all seam allowances away from the center. Be careful when pressing so you do not distort the unit. Measure the unit after adding and pressing each round of border strips to keep the quilt top accurate. Square the quilt top if needed. Each complete border round will add 1" to the measurement.

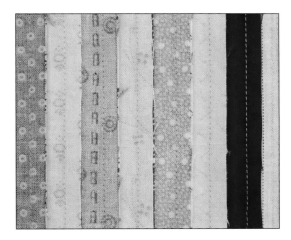

Press all seam allowances away from the center square to keep the bulk all going one way.

6. Sew red-leaf 2" x 15½" strips to opposite sides of the unit. Press the seam allowances away from the center.

7. Sew red-leaf 2" x 18½" strips to the top and bottom of the unit. Press the seam allowances away from the center.

Finishing the Quilt

For more detailed information about any finishing steps, visit ShopMartingale.com/HowtoQuilt.

1. Layer the quilt top, batting, and backing. Baste the layers together.

2. Hand or machine quilt as desired. The quilt shown is machine quilted with a diagonal crosshatch grid in both the center toile print square and the outer border. The narrow borders are all quilted in the ditch.

3. Use the tan 1⅛"-wide strips to make and attach single-fold binding. For more detailed information on my technique for making and attaching the binding, see "Single-Fold Binding" on page 78.

4. Make and attach a hanging sleeve, if desired.

5. Make, sign, and date a label and attach it to your quilt.

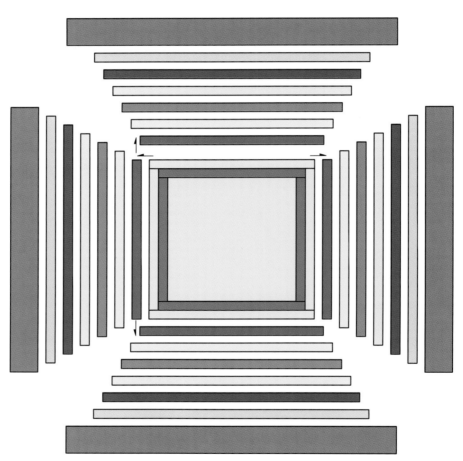

Quilt assembly

Creating interesting vignettes throughout my home that allow me to easily change quilts and a few key decorations is one of my favorite tricks. One-of-a-kind display items, such as an old painted door, suits this idea perfectly. Pin your quilt to the propped up door, hang a filled basket on the doorknob, and place seasonal decor atop an iron urn. What a welcoming display that's easy to adapt all year.

Materials

Yardage is based on 42"-wide fabric. Fat quarters are 18" x 21". Fat eighths are 9" x 18".

1 fat eighth OR 9"x10" piece *each* of 4 gold prints for flying-geese units
¾ yard black print for flying-geese units, sashing, border, and binding
¾ yard of fabric for backing
26" x 32" piece of batting

Cutting

From the assorted gold prints, cut a *total* of:
11 squares, 4¼" x 4¼"

From the *crosswise* grain of the black print, cut:
3 strips, 1⅛" x 42", for binding

From the remaining black print, cut:
44 squares, 2⅜" x 2⅜"
6 strips, 3½" x 21½"

Making the Flying-Geese Units

1. Draw a diagonal line from corner to corner on the wrong side of the 44 black 2⅜" squares.

2. Align two marked squares on opposite corners of a gold 4¼" square, right sides together. Note the squares will overlap in the center. Sew a scant ¼" from each side of the drawn lines.

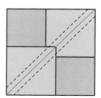

MARKING ON BLACK FABRIC

To mark lines clearly on the wrong side of the black-print squares, I recommend using a Clover fine-point White Marking Pen #517 to draw the lines. The lines will disappear with the touch of a hot iron or water. I use this pen to mark quilting lines for hand or machine quilting.

FINISHED QUILT: 21½" x 27½"

3. Cut the unit apart on the drawn lines. Press the seam allowances toward the small triangles.

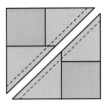 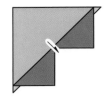

4. Align one black 2⅜" square on the corner of the large triangle. Note that the direction of the diagonal line is toward the center. Sew a scant ¼" from each side of the drawn line.

5. Cut the unit apart on the drawn line. Press the seam allowances toward the small black triangles to make a flying-geese unit. Repeat with the remaining pieces to make a total of four flying-geese units. Square these units to measure 2" x 3½".

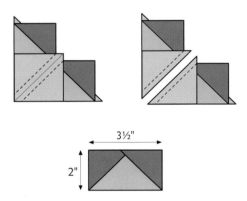

6. Repeat steps 2–5 to make a total of 44 flying-geese units. You'll only use 42 in this project.

Assembling the Wall-Hanging Top

1. Lay out 14 flying-geese units in a vertical row, noting the direction of the flying-geese points.

2. Sew the units together. Carefully press the seam allowances away from the flying-geese points. Do not stretch the row. The row should measure 21½" long.

3. Repeat steps 1 and 2 to make a total of three flying-geese rows.

4. Lay out the flying-geese rows and two black 3½" x 21½" sashing strips. Pin and sew the rows and sashing strips together. Press the seam allowances toward the sashing strips. Your quilt top should measure 15½" x 21½".

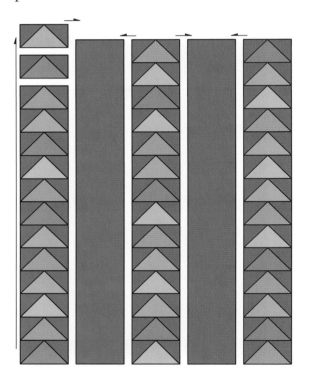

5. Sew two black 3½" x 21½" strips to the sides of the quilt top. Press the seam allowances toward the border.

6. Pin and sew the two remaining black 3½" x 21½" strips to the top and bottom of the quilt top. Press the seam allowances toward the border.

Finishing the Wall Hanging

For more detailed information about any finishing steps, visit ShopMartingale.com/HowtoQuilt.

1. Layer the quilt top, batting, and backing. Baste the layers together.

2. Hand or machine quilt as desired. The quilt shown is machine quilted with gold thread in an allover diagonal crosshatching pattern that aligns with the angles of the geese and continues into the border.

3. Use the black 1⅛"-wide strips to make and attach single-fold binding. For more detailed information on my technique for making and attaching the binding, see "Single-Fold Binding" on page 78.

4. Make and attach a hanging sleeve, if desired.

5. Make, sign, and date a label and attach it to your quilt.

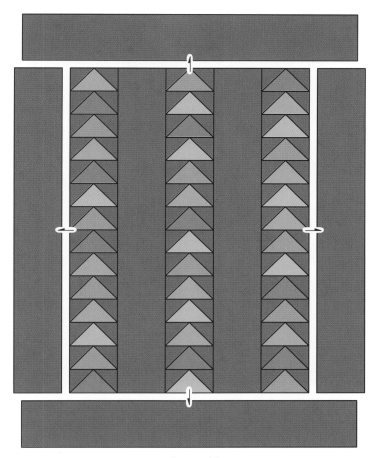

Quilt assembly

Materials

Yardage is based on 42"-wide fabric. Fat eighths are 9" x 21".

1 fat eighth or scrap *each* of 9 dark prints for blocks
1 fat eighth or scrap *each* of 9 light prints for blocks
¾ yard of brown print for sashing and outer border
¼ yard of brown-and-cream stripe for inner border
1 fat quarter *OR* ¼ yard of light-brown print for
 binding
¾ yard of fabric for backing
27" x 27" piece of batting

Cutting

Cut the sashing and outer-border strips from the lengthwise grain (parallel to the selvages); strips cut crosswise have more stretch. Carefully cut the inner-border strips crosswise to achieve the desired stripe.

From *each* dark-print fat eighth or scrap, cut:
9 squares, 1½" x 1½" (81 total)

From *each* light-print fat eighth or scrap, cut:
4 squares, 1½" x 1½" (36 total)
2 squares, 2¾" x 2¾"; cut each square into quarters
 diagonally to yield 8 setting triangles (72 total)
2 squares, 2" x 2"; cut each square in half diagonally
 to yield 4 corner triangles (36 total)

From the *lengthwise* grain of the brown print, cut:
2 strips, 2½" x 18¼"
2 strips, 2½" x 22¼"
6 strips, 1½" x 4¾"
4 strips, 1½" x 15¼"
2 strips, 1½" x 17¼"

From the *crosswise* grain of the brown-and-cream stripe, cut:
2 strips, 1" x 17¼"
2 strips, 1" x 18¼"

From the *crosswise* grain of the light-brown print, cut:
6 strips, 1⅛" x 21", for binding

A quilt can enhance or decorate your cupboards in a number of ways. Antique cupboards offer great display potential. Fold a little quilt and drape it over one door. On taller cupboards, it keeps small quilts at eye level, without having to hang them flat against the wall. By folding the quilt so it is slightly smaller than the door, you visually frame your quilt, making it pop off the background.

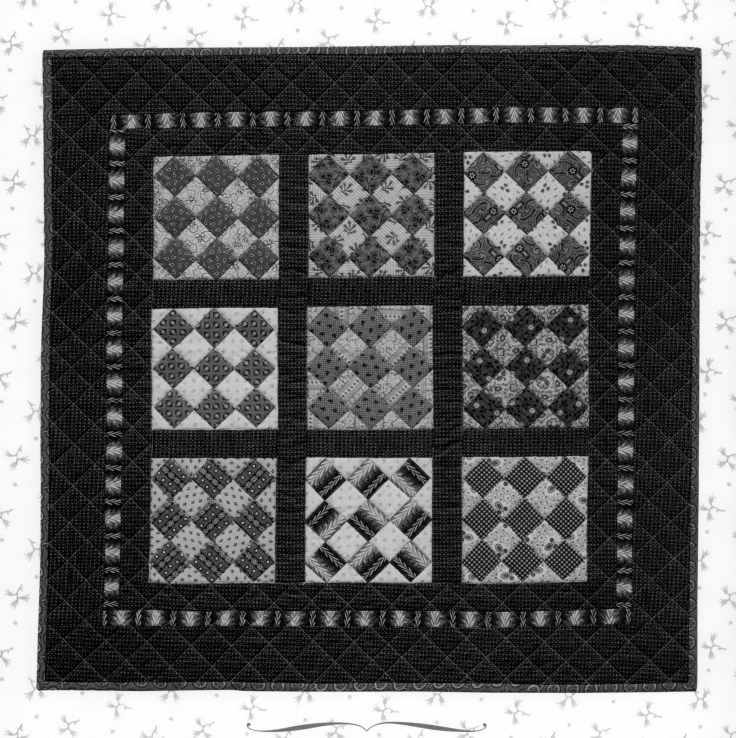

FINISHED QUILT: 22¼" x 22¼" ✂ FINISHED BLOCK: 4¼" x 4¼"

Making the Blocks

1. Gather nine 1½" squares from one dark print and four 1½" squares, eight setting triangles, and four corner triangles from one light print.

2. Lay out the dark squares, light squares, and light setting triangles in five diagonal rows. Note that the dark and light squares will be on point.

3. Sew the pieces in each row together using a scant ¼" seam allowance. Press the seam allowances toward the dark-print squares.

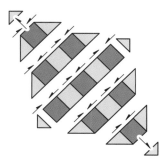

4. Pin and sew the rows together, matching seam intersections. Add the light corner triangles; press the seam allowances toward the triangles. Refer to "Clipping Trick" on page 78 and continue pressing toward the dark fabric.

Use my clipping trick to press seam intersections into little four patches for a smooth quilt top.

5. Trim the setting triangles and corner triangles (they were cut slightly oversize), being sure to leave a ¼" seam allowance beyond the points. Square the block to measure 4¾" x 4¾".

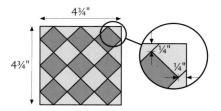

6. Repeat steps 1–5 to make a total of nine Nine Patch Checkerboard blocks.

Assembling the Quilt Top

1. Lay out the Nine Patch Checkerboard blocks, six brown 1½" x 4¾" sashing strips, and four brown 1½" x 15¼" sashing strips in seven horizontal rows.

2. Sew the blocks and 4¾"-long sashing strips together to make three block rows. Press the seam allowances toward the sashing.

3. Sew the 15¼"-long sashing strips and the blocks rows together as shown. Press the seam allowances toward the sashing. Sew the 17¼"-long sashing strips to the remaining sides. Press the seam allowances toward the sashing. Your quilt top should measure 17¼" x 17¼".

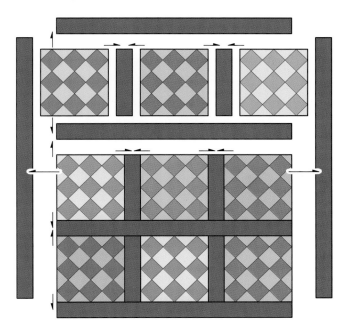

4. Sew the brown-and-cream stripe 1" x 17¼" strips to the top and bottom of the quilt. Press the seam allowances toward the inner border. Sew the brown-and-cream stripe 1" x 18¼" strips to the remaining sides of the quilt. Press the seam allowances toward the inner border.

5. Sew the brown 2½" x 18¼" strips to the top and bottom of the quilt. Press the seam allowances toward the outer border. Sew the brown 2½" x 22¼" strips to the remaining sides. Press the seam allowances toward the outer border.

Finishing the Quilt

For more detailed information about any finishing steps, visit ShopMartingale.com/HowtoQuilt.

1. Layer the quilt top, batting, and backing. Baste the layers together.

2. Hand or machine quilt as desired. The quilt shown is machine quilted in a diagonal crosshatch grid, following the outlines of the patches in the Nine Patch Checkerboard blocks.

3. Use the light-brown 1⅛"-wide strips to make and attach the single-fold binding. For more detailed information on my technique for making and attaching the binding, see "Single-Fold Binding" on page 78.

4. Make and attach a hanging sleeve, if desired.

5. Make, sign, and date a label and attach it to your quilt.

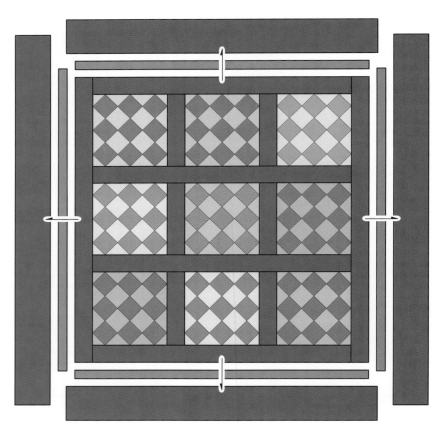

Quilt assembly

Indigo Stars Doll Quilt

Tuck quilts in unexpected places where you'll get to enjoy them when you happen upon them. That's how this little charmer ended up as the folded liner of a sewing basket. You may not see it until you pass by, but when you do, it's sure to bring a smile to your face. Inspired by an antique indigo-and-muslin doll quilt that I saw in Pennsylvania, its unexpected green-print binding matches the original.

Materials

Yardage is based on 42"-wide fabric. Fat quarters are 18" x 21".

4 fat quarters of indigo prints for blocks
3 fat quarters of tan-and-blue *OR* beige-and-blue prints for blocks
1 fat quarter of green print for binding
1 fat quarter of fabric for backing
17" x 17" piece of batting

Cutting

For each *of the 5 star blocks with light backgrounds*

From the indigo prints, cut:
4 squares, 1⅞" x 1⅞" (20 total)

From the tan-and-blue *or* beige-and-blue prints, cut:
4 squares, 1½" x 1½" (20 total)
1 square, 2½" x 2½" (5 total)
1 square, 3¼" x 3¼" (5 total)

For each *of the 4 star blocks with dark backgrounds*

From the indigo prints, cut:
4 squares, 1½" x 1½" (16 total)
1 square, 2½" x 2½" (4 total)
1 square, 3¼" x 3¼" (4 total)

From the tan-and-blue prints *or* beige-and-blue prints, cut:
4 squares, 1⅞" x 1⅞" (16 total)

For assembling the quilt top

From the *crosswise* grain of the green print, cut:
4 strips, 1⅛" x 21", for binding

FINISHED QUILT: 12½" x 12½" ✄ FINISHED BLOCK: 4" x 4"

Making the Blocks

1. Draw a diagonal line from corner to corner on the wrong side of the indigo 1⅞" squares and the tan-and-blue or beige-and-blue 1⅞" squares.

2. Align two marked indigo squares on opposite corners of the tan-and-blue or beige-and-blue 3¼" square, right sides together. Note the squares will overlap in the center. Sew a scant ¼" from each side of the drawn lines.

3. Cut the unit apart on the drawn lines. Press the seam allowances toward the small triangles.

4. Align one indigo 1⅞" square on the corner of the large tan-and-blue or beige-and-blue triangle. Note that the direction of the diagonal line is toward the center. Sew a scant ¼" from each side of the drawn line. Cut the unit apart on the drawn line. Press the seam allowances toward the small triangles to make a flying-geese unit. Repeat with remaining pieces to make a total of four matching flying-geese units. Trim the units to measure 1½" x 2½".

5. Lay out four tan-and-blue or beige-and-blue 1½" squares and one 2½" square and the flying-geese units in three rows. Sew the squares and units into rows. Press the seam allowances toward the squares.

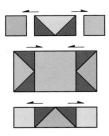

6. Pin and sew the rows together, matching seam intersections, to make a Sawtooth Star block with a light background. Press the seam allowances toward the middle row.

7. Repeat steps 2–6 to make a total of five Sawtooth Star blocks with a light background.

8. Repeat steps 2–6 using the marked tan-and-blue or beige-and-blue 1⅞" squares and remaining indigo squares to make a total of four Sawtooth Star blocks with dark backgrounds. Press the seam allowances toward the top and bottom rows (this will help you nest the seams of the alternating light and dark blocks when you assemble the quilt top).

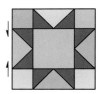 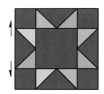

Make 5.   Make 4.

9. Refer to "Clipping Trick" on page 78 to clip at the four seam intersections for each block. Press the flying-geese units toward the center, press the squares toward the corners, and press the seam

intersections open. Each Sawtooth Star block should measure 4½" x 4½". Trim as needed.

Assembling the Quilt Top

1. Arrange the Sawtooth Star blocks in three rows of three blocks each, alternating light and dark backgrounds.

2. Sew the blocks in each row together. Press the seam allowances open.

3. Pin the rows together, matching the seam intersections. Sew the rows together. Press the seam allowances open.

Finishing the Quilt

For more detailed information about any finishing steps, visit ShopMartingale.com/HowtoQuilt.

1. Layer the quilt top, batting, and backing. Baste the layers together.

2. Hand or machine quilt as desired. I hand quilted each Sawtooth Star block in the ditch along the seam lines. Then I stitched an *X* in the center square and corner square of each block, adding a perpendicular line to divide the large triangle of each flying-geese unit.

3. Use the green 1⅛"-wide strips to make and attach single-fold binding. For more detailed information on my technique for making and attaching the binding, see "Single-Fold Binding" on page 78.

4. Make and attach a hanging sleeve, if desired.

5. Make, sign, and date a label and attach it to your quilt.

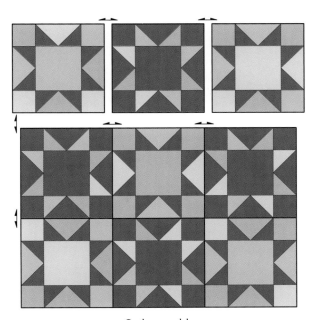

Quilt assembly

Materials

Yardage is based on 42"-wide fabric. Fat eighths are 9" x 21". Fat quarters are 18" x 21".

8 fat eighths or scraps of assorted medium prints for blocks

8 fat eighths or scraps of assorted dark prints for blocks

¾ yard of brown stripe for sashing strips

¾ yard of cream print for border

½ yard of light print for blocks

½ yard of pink floral for setting triangles

1 fat quarter of brown floral for border cornerstones

1 fat quarter OR ¼ yard of pink print for single-fold binding

1 yard of fabric for backing

30" x 36" piece of batting

Cutting

Cut the sashing strips from the lengthwise grain (parallel to the selvages) to achieve the desired stripe. For each block, use at least three fabrics: one for the basket, one for the background, and one for the triangles (flowers). For a scrappier version, use more than one fabric for the flowers.

The following cutting instructions for the background fabric, basket, and flowers are for one block. Repeat to cut pieces to make a total of eight blocks.

From the light print, cut:

1 square, 2⅞" x 2⅞"; cut in half diagonally to yield 2 large triangles (You will use 1 below the basket bottom; 1 will be left over for the next block.)

3 squares, 1⅞" x 1⅞"

1 square, 1⅞" x 1⅞"; cut in half diagonally to yield 2 small triangles

2 rectangles, 1½" x 2½"

From 1 medium print, cut:

3 squares, 1⅞" x 1⅞"

Continued on page 49

Consider the popularity of gallery walls, then imagine how small quilts can be incorporated into the mix with dissimilar items. Quilts as wall hangings don't have to be lonely. Pair them with a favorite shelf and a table below them. Here, eye-catching sashing strips counterbalance an array of florals flowing in the baskets, backgrounds, and borders. Those fabrics inspired the garden-themed accessories.

FINISHED QUILT: 25¼" x 31¼" ✄ FINISHED BLOCK: 4" x 4"

Continued from page 47

From 1 dark print, cut:

1 square, 1⅞" x 1⅞"; cut in half diagonally to yield 2 small triangles for the basket feet

1 square, 2⅞" x 2⅞"; cut in half diagonally to yield 2 large triangles (You will use 1 for the basket; 1 will be left over.)

From the pink floral, cut:

3 squares, 7" x 7"; cut each square into quarters diagonally to yield 12 setting triangles

4 squares, 4" x 4"; cut each square in half diagonally to yield 8 corner triangles

From the *lengthwise* grain of the brown stripe, cut:

3 strips, 2¼" x 23¼"

From the cream print, cut:

2 strips, 4½" x 23⅛"

2 strips, 4½" x 17"

From the brown floral, cut:

4 squares, 4½" x 4½"

From the *crosswise* grain of the pink print, cut:

6 strips, 1⅛" x 21", for binding

Making the Blocks

1. Draw a diagonal line from corner to corner on the wrong side of three matching light-print 1⅞" squares.

2. Lay a marked light-print square on top of a medium-print 1⅞" square, right sides together. Sew a scant ¼" from each side of the drawn line. Cut the unit apart on the drawn line to make two half-square-triangle units. Repeat to make six half-square-triangle units. Press the seam allowances toward the medium-print triangle. Trim each unit to measure 1½" x 1½".

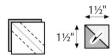

3. Lay out the half-square-triangle units, two small triangles, two rectangles, and one large triangle from the same light print used in the units, and two small triangles and one large triangle from the same dark print.

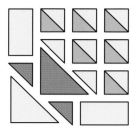

4. Join the small light-print triangles and the half-square-triangle units in three rows, noting the orientation of the medium-print triangles. Press the seam allowances in the first and third row toward the medium-print triangles and press the seam allowances in the middle row toward the light-print triangles.

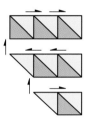

5. Join the rows together, matching intersections. Press the seam allowances toward the medium-print triangles.

6. Join the large dark-print triangle to the unit from step 6 to make the basket body. Press the seam allowances toward the large triangle. The square should measure 3½" x 3½".

7. Join a small dark-print triangle to one end of each light-print 1½" x 2½" rectangle to make the basket feet. Press the seam allowances toward dark triangles.

8. Sew the basket feet to the basket body. Press the seam allowances toward the basket feet. Center

the large light-print triangle at the base of the basket feet, pin, and sew together to make a basket block. Press the seam allowances toward the large light-print triangle. The block should measure 4½" x 4½".

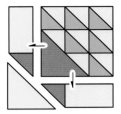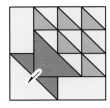

9. Repeat steps 1–8 to make a total of eight Basket blocks.

Assembling the Quilt Top

1. Lay out four basket blocks, six pink-floral setting triangles, and four pink-floral corner triangles in a vertical row with the basket blocks set on-point.

2. Sew the setting triangles to the sides of the blocks; then center and sew the corner triangles to the top and bottom blocks in each row. Press the seam allowances toward the triangles.

3. Pin the units together, matching the seam intersections. Sew the units together to make a basket row. Press the seam allowances toward the triangles, referring to "Clipping Trick" on page 78. The setting and corner triangles were cut slightly oversized. Trim the triangles, leaving a ¼" seam allowance beyond the points. Square each basket row to measure 6¼" x 23¼".

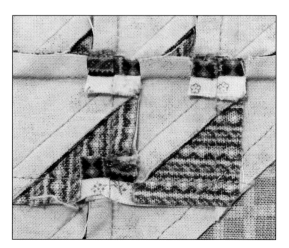

Using my clipping trick at seam intersections really helps reduce the bulk.

4. Repeat steps 1–3 to make a second basket row.

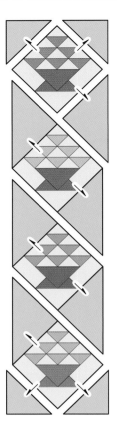

5. Pin and sew the brown-striped sashing strips to the basket rows. Press the seam allowances toward the sashing strips. Trim the quilt center to 17" x 23⅛".

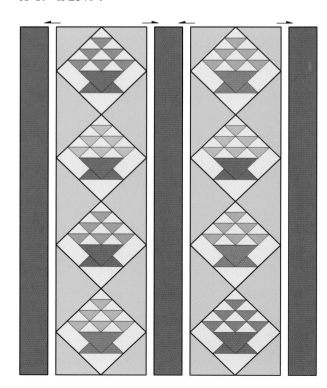

6. Sew the cream 4½" x 23⅛" strips to each long side of the quilt top. Press the seam allowances toward the border.

7. Sew the brown-floral 4½" squares to each end of the remaining cream 4½" x 17" strips. Press the seam allowances toward the strips. Pin and sew the border strips, matching the seam intersections, to the top and bottom of the quilt top. Press the seam allowances toward the border. Referring to "Clipping Trick," press the clipped intersections open to form a small four patch on the back of the quilt top.

Finishing the Quilt

For more detailed information about any finishing steps, visit ShopMartingale.com/HowtoQuilt.

1. Layer the quilt top, batting, and backing. Baste the layers together.

2. Hand or machine quilt as desired. The quilt shown is machine quilted in the ditch around the pieces in the basket blocks. The setting triangles are echo quilted in a series of three lines while the striped sashing strips are quilted with parallel vertical lines. The border is filled with fancy feather quilting, which makes a nice counterpoint to all the straight-line quilting in the interior.

3. Use the pink 1⅛"-wide strips to make and attach single-fold binding. For more detailed information on my technique for making and attaching the binding, see "Single-Fold Binding" on page 78.

4. Make and attach a hanging sleeve, if desired.

5. Make, sign, and date a label and attach it to your quilt.

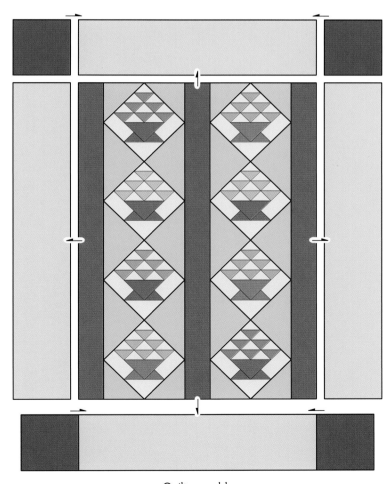

Quilt assembly

Materials

Yardage is based on 42"-wide fabric. Fat quarters are 18" x 21". Fat eighths are 9" x 18".

Scraps (about ½ yard total) of assorted light and medium prints for block logs

Scraps (about ¼ yard total) of assorted dark prints for block logs

1 fat quarter OR ¼ yard of rust print for single-fold binding

1 fat eighth of red print for block centers

½ yard of fabric for backing

20" x 20" piece of batting

Cutting

Cut all of the logs from the lengthwise grain (parallel to the selvages), so that the blocks will lie flat. Crosswise strips have more stretch, making it more difficult to keep the blocks flat and smooth.

The number of strips you need for each dark and light print depends on the position of the strips in the block and how often the print is repeated. For each of the Log Cabin blocks, you'll need four dark and four light fabrics. For each of the Courthouse Steps blocks, you'll need four light or medium fabrics (one print for each round of logs). Start by cutting four strips of each print, and then cut more as needed.

From the red print, cut:
9 squares, 1¼" x 1¼"

From the *lengthwise* grain of the assorted light and medium prints, cut:
36 strips, at least 1" x 12" or longer

From the *lengthwise* grain of the assorted dark prints, cut:
16 strips, at least 1" x 12" or longer

From the *crosswise* grain of the rust print, cut:
4 strips, 1⅛" x 21", for binding

The Log Cabin block is one of my favorites! I was inspired to make this little topper consisting of four Log Cabin blocks and five Courthouse Steps blocks from an antique quilt that had 16 blocks. I got the same feel by making a smaller variation with only nine blocks.

Make sure your small quilt treasures can be seen from across the room by using an antique bowl or box to give one edge of the quilt a lift. It invites a closer look of the treasures that lie within.

FINISHED QUILT: 14¾" x 14¾" ✂ FINISHED BLOCK: 4¾" x 4¾"

You may like to make a runner of four or five blocks in a single row for an adorable accent piece. Another idea is to use a single block for a mug rug: With top and backing right sides together, place batting atop layers and sew around the outer edges leaving a small opening. Turn right side out, whipstitch the opening closed, and quilt a couple of rounds to hold the layers in place. What a nice gift for a sewing friend!

Making the Log Cabin Blocks

Sew the strips or "logs" around the center red square in a clockwise manner, starting with light/medium strips on the first two adjacent sides and dark strips on the remaining two sides. Follow the numbered sequence in the block diagram (above right) to sew the strips to a red 1¼" square. Use the same light/medium print for the first two strips, then switch to a dark print and use it for the next two positions. Continue using one light/medium and one dark print per round to make the block. Place the strip beneath the square or unit for sewing. It's important to use an accurate ¼"-wide seam allowance to make the blocks finish to the same size.

1. Select four dark and four light or medium strips for each of the four Log Cabin blocks as follows.

   Round 1:
   light or medium print #1 for positions 1 and 2; dark print #1 for positions 3 and 4

   Round 2:
   light or medium print #2 for positions 5 and 6; dark print #2 for positions 7 and 8

   Round 3:
   light or medium print #3 for positions 9 and 10; dark print #3 for positions 11 and 12

   Round 4:
   light or medium print #4 for positions 13 and 14; dark print #4 for positions 15 and 16

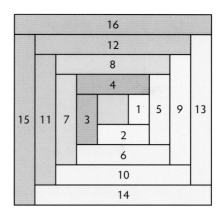

Log Cabin block

2. Sew a red 1¼" square to one end of a light or medium #1 strip, right sides together. Press to set the seam, and then press the seam allowances away from the red square (see "Press, Don't Iron" on page 56). Using a rotary cutter and mat and an acrylic ruler, trim the ends of the strip even with the red square.

3. Align the remainder of the light or medium #1 strip with the bottom edge of the unit from step 2, right sides together and at the end of the strip. Sew together; press to set the seam, and then press the seam allowances away from the square. Trim the strip ends even with the unit.

4. Align a dark #1 strip with the left side of the unit from step 3, right sides together. Sew, press, and trim as before.

5. Align the remainder of the dark #1 strip with the top of the unit from step 4, right sides together and at the end of the strip. Sew, press, and trim as before. You now have added logs to all four sides of the unit, completing round 1. Square the unit to 2¼" x 2¼".

6. Continue to add three additional rounds of dark and light or medium strips in clockwise rotation around the unit. Sew, press, and trim each strip as before. Square the unit to 5¼" x 5¼" to make a Log Cabin block.

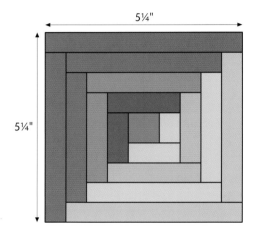

5¼"

5¼"

7. Repeat steps 2–6 to make a total of four Log Cabin blocks.

PRESS, DON'T IRON

As you sew together the strips (logs) to assemble the blocks, first press to set the seam, and then press the strip *away* from the center. When you press, set the iron over the seam and lift it up; do not slide the iron across the seam or your seams may bow outward.

Important! Use your ruler and rotary cutter to trim the ends and keep the unit straight and square.

Making the Courthouse Steps Blocks

Unlike a Log Cabin block, the logs in a Courthouse Steps block are added to *opposite* sides of the center square first, then added to the two remaining sides. In these blocks, each round of logs will use one light or medium strip for all four sides of the round. Follow the numbered sequence shown in the block diagram below to add the strips to a red 1¼" square. Place the strip beneath the square or unit for sewing. It's important to use an accurate ¼"-wide seam allowance to make the blocks finish to the same size.

1. Select four light or medium strips for each of the five Courthouse Steps blocks as follows. Follow the numbered strips in the block diagram to make each Courthouse Steps block, placing each strip under the center square unit to sew them together.

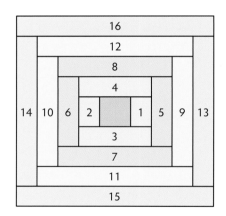

Courthouse Steps block

2. Sew a red 1¼" square to one end of a light or medium #1 strip, right sides together, with the square on top. Press to set the seam, and then press the seam allowances away from the red square. Using a rotary cutter and mat and an acrylic ruler, trim the ends of light- or medium-print strip even with the red square.

3. In the same manner, sew a matching light or medium #1 strip to the opposite side of the red square. Press and trim as before.

4. Sew a matching light or medium #1 strip to the top edge of the unit. Press and trim as before. Sew the remaining matching light or medium #1 strip to the bottom edge of the unit. Press and trim. You now have added one round of matching strips to four sides. Square the unit to measure 2¼" x 2¼".

   Note: Be careful when pressing that you do not distort the unit. Measure the unit after adding and pressing each round of strips to keep the quilt top accurate. Square the quilt top if needed. Each complete round of strips will add 1" to the measurement.

5. In the same manner, continue to add the light- or medium-print strips in sequence to opposite sides of the unit to make a Courthouse Steps block. Sew, press, and trim each strip as before. The block should measure 5¼" x 5¼".

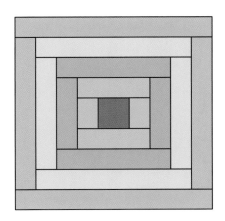

6. Repeat steps 2–5 to make a total of five Courthouse Steps blocks.

Assembling the Quilt Top

1. Arrange the Log Cabin and Courthouse Steps blocks in three rows of three blocks each, rotating the Log Cabin blocks so the dark prints are on the outer edges of the quilt top.

2. Sew the blocks in each row together. Press the seam allowances open.

3. Pin and sew the rows, matching the seam intersections. Press the seam allowances open.

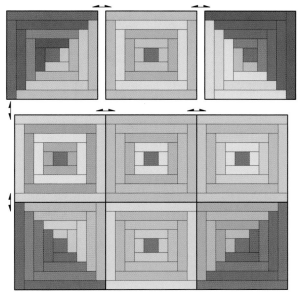

Quilt assembly

Finishing the Quilt

For more detailed information about any finishing steps, visit ShopMartingale.com/HowtoQuilt.

1. Layer the quilt top, batting, and backing. Baste the layers together.

2. Hand or machine quilt as desired. I hand quilted in concentric squares about ⅛" from the ditch so the quilting can be seen. You will have double quilting about ¼" apart where the blocks are joined.

3. Use the rust 1⅛"-wide strips to make and attach single-fold binding. For more detailed information on my technique for making and attaching the binding, see "Single-Fold Binding" on page 78.

4. Make and attach a hanging sleeve, if desired.

5. Make, sign, and date a label and attach it to your quilt.

Materials

Yardage is based on 42"-wide fabric. Fat quarters are 18" x 21".

⅓ yard *total* of assorted light prints for blocks, setting triangles, and corner triangles

⅓ yard *total* of assorted dark prints for blocks, setting triangles, and corner triangles

1 fat quarter of tan print for blocks, setting triangles, and corner triangles

1 yard of brown print for sashing

1 fat quarter OR ¼ yard of black print for single-fold binding

¾ yard of fabric for backing

24" x 30" piece of batting

Cutting

From the assorted light prints, cut:

48 squares, 1¾" x 1¾"; cut 36 of the squares in matching pairs

From the assorted dark prints, cut:

48 squares, 1¾" x 1¾"; cut 36 of the squares in matching pairs

From the tan print, cut:

41 squares, 2¾" x 2¾"; cut each square in half diagonally to yield 82 large triangles

7 squares, 3" x 3"; cut each square into quarters diagonally to yield 28 small triangles

From the brown print, cut:

24 strips, 1½" x 4"

2 strips, 1½" x 6"

2 strips, 1½" x 15"

2 strips, 1½" x 24"

1 strip, 1½" x 30"

From the *crosswise* grain of the black print, cut:

6 strips, 1⅛" x 21", for binding

Borderless quilts are ideal as table toppers. But don't restrict yourself to placing decor in the center. A bit of asymmetry can add interest and give the quilt a chance to shine.

For even more interest, don't strip piece all the blocks in your quilt. You'll get more variety and fabric mixes that way. And don't worry about lining up all the plaids and stripes. Just let them fall where they may.

FINISHED QUILT: 19½" x 26" ✄ FINISHED BLOCK: 3½" x 3½"

Making the Blocks

1. Using matching light and dark pairs of 1¾" squares, sew each light square to a dark square to make two matching units. Press the seam allowances toward the dark square. Repeat with the remaining sets of matching light and dark 1¾" squares to make a total of 36 segments.

   To save sewing time, chain sew the fabric squares by inserting each pair under the presser foot, one right after another, without clipping the threads between the pairs. You'll clip the threads to separate the pairs once all the fabric pairs have been sewn together.

2. Pin and sew together two matching segments, matching the seam intersections, to make a four-patch unit. Press the seam allowances open. The four-patch unit should measure 3" x 3". Repeat to make a total of 18 four-patch units.

3. Sew the long sides of two large tan triangles to opposite sides of a four-patch unit. Press the seam allowances toward the triangles. Sew the long sides of two more large tan triangles to the remaining sides of the four-patch unit to make a Four-Patch-in-a-Square block. Press as before. Square the block to measure 4" x 4" (see "How to Square a Block," **above right**).

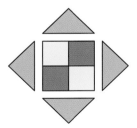 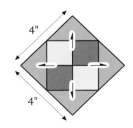

4. Repeat step 3 to make a total of 18 Four-Patch-in-a-Square blocks.

HOW TO SQUARE A BLOCK

Using a 4" or a 4½" acrylic ruler, align the 2" line both vertically and horizontally across the Four-Patch-in-a-Square block. This will be centered so you can use a rotary cutter to trim two sides of the block. Rotate the block 180°, align the ruler again as before, and trim the remaining two sides of the block.

Making the Setting Triangles

1. Sew a light 1¾" square and a dark 1¾" square together side by side. Press the seam allowances toward the dark square. Repeat with remaining light and dark 1¾" squares to make a total of 10 units.

2. Sew the long edge of a large tan triangle to one long edge of each pieced unit from step 1. Press the seam allowances toward the triangles. Note the orientation of the lights and darks (see photo on page 60) in the Four-Patch-in-a-Square blocks and the setting triangles before adding the small tan triangles to these segments.

3. Sew a short edge of a small tan triangle to one short end of the unit from step 2. Sew another small tan triangle to the opposite side of the unit to make a setting triangle. Press the seam allowances toward the triangles. Check the orientation of each small triangle before you sew it to the segment; the long side of the small triangle becomes the inside edge of the setting triangle.

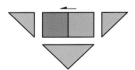 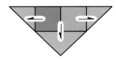

4. Repeat steps 2 and 3 to make a total of 10 setting triangles.

Making the Corner Triangles

1. Sew the short side of a small tan triangle to one side of a light or dark 1¾" square. Press the seam allowances toward the triangle. Sew the short side of a second small tan triangle to the adjacent side of the unit from step 1 to make a corner triangle. Press the seam allowances toward the triangle. The long sides of the small tan triangles become the long edge of the corner block.

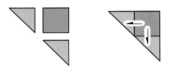

2. Repeat step 1 to make a total of four corner triangles—two with light-print squares and two with dark-print squares.

Assembling the Quilt Top

1. Lay out the blocks, sashing strips, setting triangles, and corner triangles in diagonal rows on a design wall or other flat surface. Be sure the dark prints in the Four-Patch-in-a-Square blocks are all going in the same direction. Arrange the setting triangles around the outside edge noting the position of the dark prints. Place the corner triangles and again note that the placement of light and dark prints are in opposite corners, echoing the Four-Patch-in-a-Square placement.

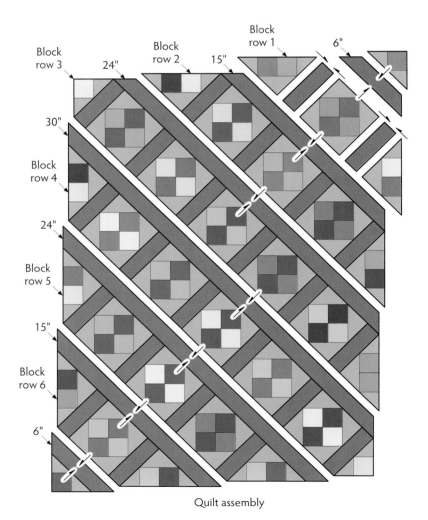

Quilt assembly

2. Sew together blocks, setting triangles, and brown 1½" x 4" sashing strips in each diagonal block row to make six block rows total. Press the seam allowances toward the sashing strips.

3. Center and pin a brown 1½" x 6" sashing strip to the short side of block row 1, leaving a ¼" seam allowance extending past the shorter sashing on both ends. Sew the rows and sashing together; press the seam allowances toward the sashing strips.

4. Center and pin a corner triangle to the unit from step 3. Sew and press as before.

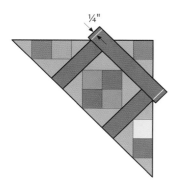

5. Pin a brown 1½" x 15" sashing strip to the short side of block row 2, leaving a ¼" seam allowance extending past the short sashing on both ends. Sew the rows and sashing together and press the seam allowances toward the sashing.

6. Pin the unit from step 4 to the unit from step 5, aligning the short sashing strips. Sew the units together. Press the seam allowances toward the sashing. (The ends of the long sashing strips will be trimmed later.)

7. Continue in this same manner, adding a brown long sashing strip to the adjacent block row, and then joining the pieced unit to the previously assembled units, to make the quilt top.

8. Using a long acrylic ruler and rotary cutter, trim the quilt top to measure 19½" x 26", carefully trimming away the ends of the long sashing strips and being sure to leave a ¼" seam allowance.

Finishing the Quilt

For more detailed information about finishing your quilt, visit ShopMartingale.com/HowtoQuilt.

1. Layer the quilt top, batting, and backing. Baste the layers together.

2. Hand or machine quilt as desired. I quilted an edge-to-edge grid design, starting at the top left corner and stitching to bottom right corner. Each line of stitching crossed through the blocks, creating an X in each four-patch square.

3. Use the black 1⅛"-wide strips to make and attach single-fold binding. For more detailed information on my technique for making and attaching the binding, see "Single-Fold Binding" on page 78.

4. Make, sign, and date a label and attach it to your quilt.

Materials

Yardage is based on 42"-wide fabric. Fat quarters are 18" x 21". Fat eighths are 9" x 18".

30 fat eighths *OR* scraps of assorted black prints for blocks
30 fat eighths *OR* scraps of assorted orange prints for blocks
⅓ yard of tan print for setting squares
¼ yard of gray print for setting triangles and corner triangles
1 fat quarter *OR* ¼ yard of black print for single-fold binding
¾ yard of fabric for backing
27" x 30" piece of batting

Cutting

For each block, use one black and one orange print. Keep the matching pieces together as you cut for easy piecing.

From *each* of the assorted black prints for blocks, cut:
4 squares, 1¼" x 1¼" (120 total)
1 square, 2" x 2" (30 total)

From *each* of the assorted orange prints, cut:
4 rectangles, 1¼" x 2" (120 total)

From the tan print, cut:
20 squares, 3½" x 3½"

From the gray print, cut:
5 squares, 5¾" x 5¾"; cut each square into quarters diagonally to yield 20 setting triangles (You'll need 18; 2 will be left over.)
2 squares, 3¼" x 3¼"; cut each square in half diagonally to yield 4 corner triangles

From the *crosswise* grain of the black print, cut:
4 strips, 1⅛" x 21", for binding

What's autumn without a seasonal quilt accenting your home? If you love antiques, show them off by making the background beneath them your quilts! It's more interesting than plain wood would be. Here, the mix of fabrics, textures, and wonderful small blocks are so easy to piece, it simply makes me think, "Ahhh, nothing better than this." No border makes this quilt even quicker to finish!

FINISHED QUILT: 22¼" x 26" ✄ FINISHED BLOCK: 3" x 3"

MIX-AND-MATCH FABRICS

Although the cutting list gives you what you need for one block at a time, I like to cut lots of pieces, and then lay out the blocks to be sure I like them. If any of your planned combinations don't seem to work, cut new pieces so you can mix and match fabrics until you're satisfied. I also auditioned my blocks on three different background fabrics (for the setting squares, setting triangles, and corner triangles) before I decided which ones to use. Don't be afraid to experiment—and change your mind!

Making the Blocks

1. Arrange four 1¼" squares and one 2" square from one black print, and four 1¼" x 2" rectangles from one orange print in three rows.

2. Sew the pieces in each row together. Press the seam allowances toward the black squares.

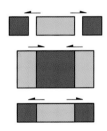

3. Pin and sew the rows together, matching the seam intersections, to make the Uneven Nine Patch block. Press the seam allowances open.

You can also press the seam allowances using the "Clipping Trick" on page 78 so the blocks will lie flat without too much bulk at the seam intersections. Press the center pieces toward the center and the corner squares toward the corners.

4. Repeat steps 1–3 to make 30 blocks.

NEATNESS COUNTS!

Look closely at how nice the back of this quilt top looks with the clipping and consistent pressing. What does the back of your quilt top look like? If the back looks nice, the front will look nice, too!

To prep for easy and smooth quilting, be sure to use my clipping trick!

Assembling the Quilt Top

1. Lay out the blocks, tan setting squares, and gray setting triangles in 10 diagonal rows as shown in the quilt assembly diagram on page 68.

2. Sew the pieces in each row together. Press the seam allowances toward the setting squares and triangles.

3. Pin and sew the rows together, matching seam intersections. Refer to "Clipping Trick" for the seam intersections. Press the seam allowances open.

4. Add the gray corner triangles; press the seam allowances toward the triangles. Trim the setting triangles and corner triangles (they were cut slightly oversize), being sure to leave a ¼" seam allowance beyond the points. Square the quilt top to measure 22¼" x 26".

Finishing the Quilt

For more detailed information about any finishing steps, visit ShopMartingale.com/HowtoQuilt.

1. Layer the quilt top, batting, and backing. Baste the layers together.

2. Hand or machine quilt as desired. The quilt shown was machine quilted in a grid of straight lines. Quilting was done in the ditch between all blocks and block pieces, which carried those lines straight through the plain setting squares.

Then the quilt was also quilted with horizontal and vertical lines intersecting the corners of all the blocks.

3. Use the black 1⅛"-wide strips to make and attach single-fold binding. For more detailed information on my technique for making and attaching the binding, see "Single-Fold Binding" on page 78.

4. Make and attach a hanging sleeve, if desired.

5. Make, sign, and date a label and attach it to your quilt.

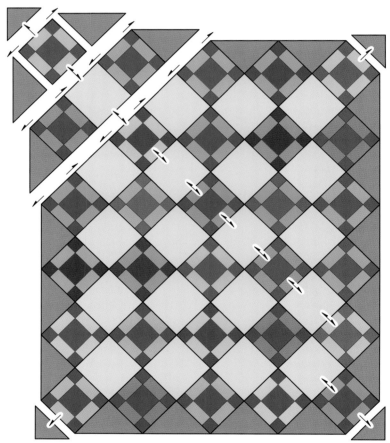

Quilt assembly

Appliquéing on a plaid background adds visual texture to this quilt. Similarly, I look for ways to add visual texture to my home by layering small quilts in the decor in unexpected places.

Do you have a small window without much of a view, or maybe a frosted window where you don't need the light to stream in? Hang a quilt over that window and improve the view! A few delicate angel vine topiaries mimic the shape of the appliqué design. Repeating elements and shapes is a design trick worth remembering.

Materials

Yardage is based on 42"-wide fabric. Fat quarters are 18" x 21".

⅔ yard of tan plaid for appliqué background

8" square of dark-red plaid for vase appliqué

⅓ yard *total* of assorted green prints for stem and leaf appliqués

¼ yard *total* of assorted yellow prints for circle appliqués

3 squares, 5" x 5", of assorted dark-red prints for star flower appliqués

⅔ yard of green print for inner border

⅝ yard of dark-red print for sawtooth outer border and binding

⅜ yard of caramel vine print for sawtooth outer border

⅔ yard of fabric for backing

25" x 33" piece of batting

Template plastic, freezer paper, or fusible web, for preparing shapes for your favorite appliqué method

Cutting

The appliqué background and inner border are cut from the lengthwise grain (parallel to the selvages) as this has the least stretch or give in a fabric. That's helpful in making your quilt accurately and results in a nice, flat quilt top. Pieces cut crosswise have more stretch.

From the *lengthwise* grain of the tan plaid, cut:
1 rectangle, 15" x 23"

From the *lengthwise* grain of the green print, cut:
2 strips, 1½" x 22½"
2 strips, 1½" x 16½"

From the *crosswise* grain of the dark-red print, cut:
3 strips, 1⅛" x 42", for binding

From the remaining dark-red print, cut:
6 squares, 6" x 6"

From the caramel vine print, cut:
6 squares, 6" x 6"

FINISHED QUILT: 20½" x 28½"

Appliquéing the Quilt Center

Use your favorite appliqué method or, if desired, refer to my tips for adding the appliqués by hand in "Needle-Turn Appliqué" on page 74, or for preparing appliqués for machine appliqué in "Using the Starch-Prep Method for Invisible Machine Appliqué" on page 75.

1. Prepare the following appliqués using patterns A–H on page 76 and referring to the materials list and photo on pages 70 and 71 for fabric colors:

   1 of A (vase)
   1 of B (stem)
   1 *each* of C and C reversed (stems)
   1 *each* of D and D reversed (stems)
   2 *each* of E and E reversed (leaves)
   1 *each* of F and F reversed (leaves)
   3 of G (star flower)
   19 of H (circles)

2. Place the appliqué shapes on the tan-plaid 15" x 23" background. Pin or baste the pieces in place.

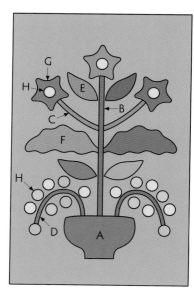

Appliqué placement diagram

3. Appliqué the shapes in place by hand or machine.

4. Trim the background to measure 14½" x 22½".

Adding the Inner Border

Sew the green 1½" x 22½" strips to the sides of the appliquéd background rectangle. Press the seam allowances toward the inner border. Sew the green 1½" x 16½" strips to the top and bottom of the background rectangle. Press the seam allowances toward the inner border.

Making the Sawtooth Outer Border

You will need a total of 44 half-square-triangle units for the outer border.

1. Draw two diagonal lines from corner to corner on the wrong side of each caramel vine-print 6" square.

2. Lay a marked caramel vine-print square on top of a dark-red 6" square right sides together. Sew a scant ¼" from each side of the drawn lines.

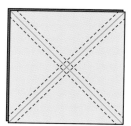

3. Cut the sewn squares apart *first* horizontally and then vertically to make four segments.

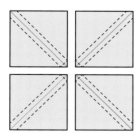

4. Cut each segment apart on the drawn diagonal line to make eight half-square-triangle units (each segment yields two half-square-triangle units). Press the seam allowances toward the dark-red triangle. Trim each unit to measure 2½" x 2½".

5. Repeat steps 2–4 to make a total of 48 half-square-triangle units. (You will use 44.)

6. Lay out 12 half-square-triangle units in a row, with the dark-red triangle toward the outer edge. Sew the units together to make a side border strip. Press the seam allowances toward the dark-red triangles. The side border strip should measure 2½" x 24½". Repeat to make a second side border strip.

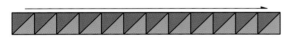

Side outer border.
Make 2.

7. Lay out 10 half-square-triangle units in a row, with the dark-red triangle toward the outer edge *except* for one unit on the left end of the row. Sew the units together to make a top border strip. Press the seam allowances toward the dark-red triangles. The top border strip should measure 2½" x 20½". Repeat to make a bottom border strip.

Top/bottom outer border.
Make 2.

8. Pin and sew the side border strips to the quilt top making sure the light triangles are adjoining the quilt top. Press the seam allowances toward the inner border. Pin and sew the top and bottom border strips to the remaining sides, again with the light triangles adjoining the quilt top. Press the seam allowances toward the inner border.

Quilt assembly

Finishing the Quilt

For more detailed information about any finishing steps, visit ShopMartingale.com/HowtoQuilt.

1. Layer the quilt top, batting, and backing. Baste the layers together.

2. Hand or machine quilt as desired. I machine quilted around each appliqué, then quilted vein accents in the leaves, a star in each flower, and horizontal lines in the vase. A meandering stitch fills in the tan-plaid background. I quilted parallel lines along the inner border and in the ditch of the outer border, adding zigzag lines to echo the sawtooth angles.

3. Use the dark-red 1⅛"-wide strips to make and attach single-fold binding. For more detailed information on my technique for making and attaching the binding, see "Single-Fold Binding" on page 78.

4. Make and attach a hanging sleeve, if desired.

5. Make, sign, and date a label and attach it to your quilt.

NEEDLE-TURN APPLIQUÉ

What You Will Need

Templates. Use freezer paper, plastic template material, or your favorite method for making templates. Trace the appliqué shape onto the selected template material. Cut out the shape with paper scissors. Remember, if your shape is directional, ask yourself if you need to reverse the template before tracing.

Marking tools. Use a marking pen (I use Clover, fine white, item #517) or a mechanical pencil (I use .7 or .9 mm lead) to draw around the template(s).

Scissors. Use a sharp pair of fabric scissors (5"-long blade is a good size; Dovo is my a favorite brand) to trim away the excess fabric, leaving about a ³⁄₁₆" or a generous ⅛" seam allowance. Pin or thread baste the appliqué pieces onto the background fabric.

Needles and thread. Thread your needle with an 18" length of matching or blending thread and knot the end. For needles, I like John James #11 Sharps or Jeana Kimball's #10 straw needles used with a Clover needle threader. The Clover Desk Needle Threader is a must-have tool!

How to Needle-Turn Appliqué

1. Beginning along a flat edge of an appliqué piece, finger-press a short area, about ½" or so, along the marked line.

2. Hold this pressed area in place with your left (or non-sewing) hand. Bring your needle out of the folded edge, leaving the knot in the fold (I don't leave knots on the back).

3. Insert the needle into the background as close to where the thread came out of the fold as possible.

4. Take a stitch about ¹⁄₁₆" wide, coming up through the folded edge of the appliqué. Barely catch the folded edge of the appliqué so the thread will not be seen.

5. After a few stitches, use your needle to gently fold and smooth the seam allowance under. It takes practice to get good at it. Turn under just enough fabric for a stitch or two or three. Don't try to turn under long areas. Avoid touching the raw edge of the fabric because it can cause fraying.

How to Stitch Inner Points

1. When you come to an inside point and you cannot turn under the fabric any more, use sharp embroidery scissors and carefully clip *to* the point. Use your needle to turn under the fabric toward the inside point. Take smaller stitches to the point.

2. When you have reached the point, turn under the seam allowance on the other side, carefully smoothing it with your needle. Making sure all threads are turned under, take an extra stitch in the inside point, and then continue up the other side, gradually increasing your stitch length from ¹⁄₁₆" to ⅛".

How to Stitch Outer Points

1. For a sharp point, stitch to the point, fold under the end at a 90° angle, and take one stitch to secure the fold. Then use your needle to turn under the other side, sweeping the fabric under

with your needle. You may need to carefully trim away excess fabric *at* the point when turning, since excess fabric can cause a rounded point and a lump.

2. Give the thread a tug to pull out the point, hold the turned-under fabric down with your thumb, and continue with the appliqué stitch.

Ending Off

1. After stitching the shape in place, insert the needle next to the appliqué edge and pull the thread to the back.

2. Wrap the thread around the needle twice, hold the needle down next to the fabric, and pull the needle and thread through to create a knot just on top of the fabric.

3. Insert your needle where the thread came out; pull to bury the knot between the background fabric and the appliqué fabric. ***Note:*** I did not cut away any of the background fabric behind the appliqués; the antique quilts I have examined had backgrounds that were left intact and were done this way.

USING THE STARCH-PREP METHOD FOR INVISIBLE MACHINE APPLIQUÉ

If hand appliqué isn't your thing, you can use invisible machine appliqué to replicate the look of handwork. I use a heat-resistant template plastic (Templar) for the starch-prep method for invisible machine appliqué. Because it's small, a travel iron is good to use for this method.

1. Trace the appliqué shapes onto the template plastic. Carefully cut them out *on* the line with your paper scissors. Be sure your edges are smooth and not jagged or rough.

2. Draw around the shape on the wrong side of the selected fabric.

3. Cut out the fabric a full ¼" larger than the drawn template line. You'll need this extra fabric to make the ironing process easier.

4. Use an inexpensive pressing pad to avoid getting starch on your ironing-board cover.

5. Spray some *heavy spray starch* in a small bowl. The heavy spray starch works best as it will turn to liquid in a short while. Using a crafts

paintbrush, apply the starch onto the ¼" seam allowance. Carefully iron the edge over the heat-resistant template plastic. You will have to do some clipping, but clip sparingly. *Only clip inside curves; never clip outside curves.*

6. Be patient; this method takes practice to become good at it, but it's worth the effort, as you need smooth edges for great machine appliqué. If you iron in a pointy tuck, crease or pleat, wet it with starch and iron again to smooth it out.

7. Set your sewing machine to a very narrow zigzag stitch; use a size 70/10 needle and 50-weight machine embroidery thread in the needle. You can use the same thread in the bobbin, or a lighter-weight thread if you prefer. Practice first on scrap fabrics to make sure you like your settings. Now you're ready to machine appliqué the prepared shapes.

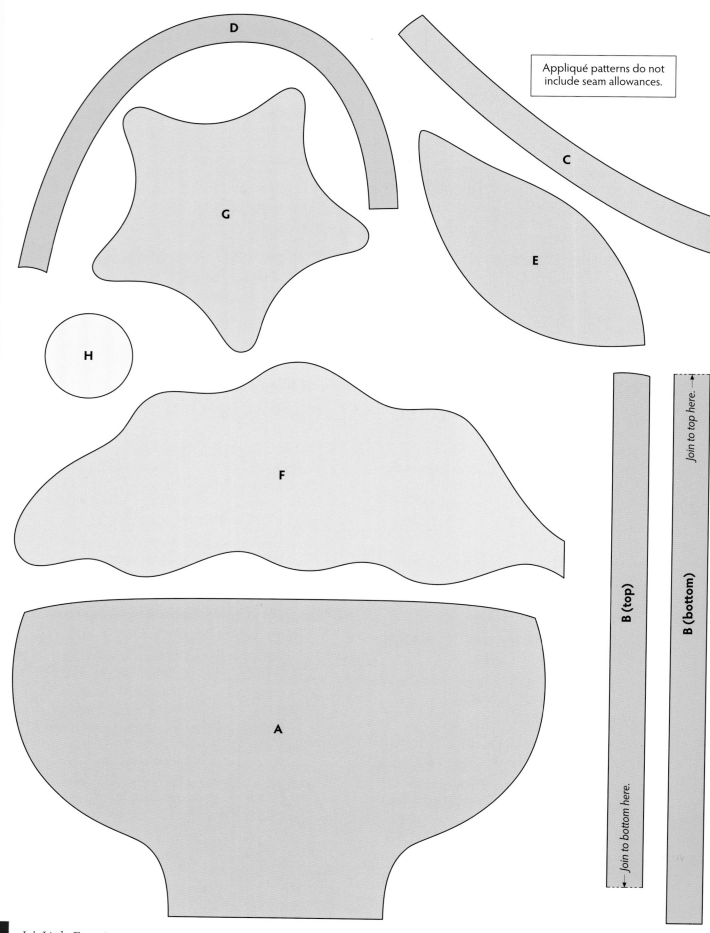

D

Appliqué patterns do not include seam allowances.

C

G

E

H

F

B (top)

Join to bottom here.

Join to top here.

B (bottom)

A

Jo's Favorite Techniques for Little Quilts

Over the years I've been asked many questions regarding how I make my little quilts. Below you'll learn how I handle things like prewashing, accurately cutting and sewing, using my clipping trick to reduce bulk and get seam intersections to lie flat, choosing batting, and applying single-fold binding. For more detailed information about rotary cutting or finishing your quilt, you can download free information at ShopMartingale.com/HowtoQuilt.

Prewashing Fabric

Do I prewash my fabrics? Yes, I do. Whether I'm sewing by hand or machine, I prefer the way prewashed fabric handles during the process of piecing or appliquéing. The fabric weave tightens up during the washing and drying process, and not only does it make it easier to handle, but it also makes it less likely to ravel as much. Prewashing also gets rid of the finish applied to fabrics, so they are softer to work with and less likely to irritate those who might be allergic to fabric finishes.

When you buy fabric, read the washing directions on the end of the bolt. Many dyes are formulated for cold water. I don't just rinse fabrics out in the sink to see if they bleed. I wash the fabric with my regular laundry soap, using the gentle wash cycle and cold water. I run it through the entire cycle and then place it in the dryer on the permanent-press setting until it's almost dry. Be careful that you do not overdry your fabric, or you will set in wrinkles. After I take it out of the dryer, I fold it immediately and place it on the shelf. I press the fabric when I'm ready to cut it for a project.

Accurate Cutting and Sewing

Accuracy is important so your blocks will come together nicely. Start with accurate cutting and continue with accurate piecing. There are several factors to consider when machine piecing to maintain accuracy.

Start by using a scant ¼" seam allowance. Why scant? When you press your seam allowances, the fold of the fabric takes up part of the seam and creates a small amount of "shrinkage." The more seams you have, the more shrinkage occurs. By sewing one or two threads less than an exact ¼", you can compensate for the fold. So, let "scant" be your friend.

Thread can also create added bulk in your seam allowances that can cause inaccuracy. A finer weight will create less bulk for flatter, more accurate seams. I prefer a 50-weight, 100% cotton thread such as Aurifil, which is a high-quality thread for hand or machine piecing. It's made from long-staple Egyptian cotton, which makes it stronger than threads that use short-staple fibers. Long-staple fibers also create less lint.

I machine piece my blocks with one of the sewing machines I own—all of which are Pfaffs. All of these machines have a dual-feed mechanism, and I engage it to keep my seams straight and my layers from shifting. It is also helpful for keeping my seams on track when sewing over seam intersections, especially diagonal seams. Before I owned these machines, I used a walking foot to keep seams straight and on track.

Clipping Trick

1. Clip up to the seamline ¼" on both sides of the seam intersection (the clips will be ½" apart). Note that the clips are lined up with the outside edge of the seam allowances.

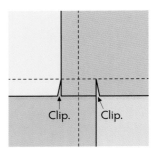

2. Now you can press each seam allowance in the direction it would like to lie and reduce the layers. See how nice and flat the top lies!

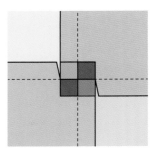

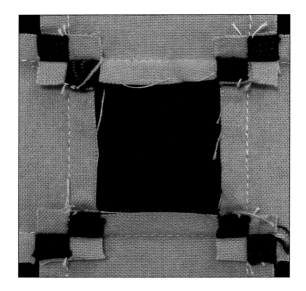

Batting

I use and recommend 100% cotton batting for these quilt projects. It drapes nicely and washes beautifully! Cotton batting also contributes to the flat, antique look and feel that I like in my finished quilts. Mountain Mist Blue Ribbon cotton batting has been my favorite for years. It needles wonderfully for hand quilting and is equally wonderful for machine quilting to achieve a vintage appearance.

Single-Fold Binding

I like a single-fold binding on all my quilts. Double-fold binding is too heavy for most small quilts and can contribute to a wavy edge. I also use a single-fold binding on my large quilts. I usually find single-fold binding on nineteenth-century quilts and believe if it was good enough for them, it is good enough for me.

To prevent the binding from stretching, I recommend using a walking foot or engaging the dual-feed mechanism, if you have one built into your machine.

1. Cut the number of 1⅛"-wide strips necessary to go around your quilt, adding 2" extra for seaming. Cut the strips crosswise (across the width of the fabric, from selvage to selvage). Using a diagonal seam, join the short ends, right sides together, to make one long piece. Press the seam allowances open.

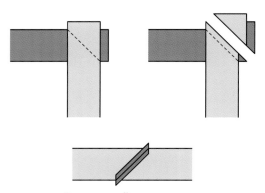

Press seam allowances open.

2. With right sides together, align a raw edge of the binding with the raw edge of the quilt. Beginning about 4" to 5" from the binding end, sew the binding to the quilt using a ¼" seam allowance.

Stop sewing ¼" from the corner; backstitch and remove the quilt from the machine.

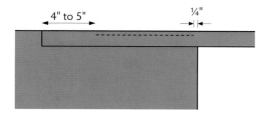

3. Rotate the quilt one quarter turn so you'll be ready to stitch the next side. Fold up the binding at a 90° angle.

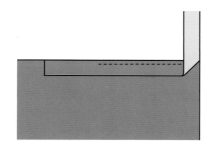

4. Next, fold the binding back down over the first fold and align the binding raw edge with the quilt raw edge. Reposition the quilt under the presser foot. Beginning with a backstitch, continue sewing the binding to the quilt top. Sew until you are ¼" from the next corner; backstitch. Repeat the folding and stitching steps at each corner.

5. Stop sewing about 5" or 6" from the start. Remove the quilt from the machine.

6. Fold the beginning of the binding strip toward the center of the quilt at a 90° angle. Repeat, folding the end of the binding strip toward the edge of the quilt at a 90° angle, leaving about a ⅛" gap between the folds. Press. By leaving the gap, the binding will lie nice and flat.

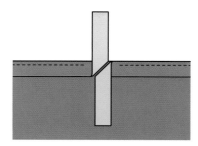

7. Align the fold lines, right sides together, and pin them in place. Sew on the fold line, backstitching at the beginning and end. Trim the excess binding strip, leaving a ¼" seam allowance. Press the seam allowances open. Finish sewing the binding in place.

8. Trim the batting and backing even with the quilt edges. Fold the binding away from the quilt and turn the raw edge under ¼". Fold the binding over the quilt edge and pin it in place so it covers the first stitches, mitering corners as you go when turning.

9. Blindstitch the binding to the quilt back, using small, closely spaced stitches and being careful not to stitch through to the front of the quilt. I recommend taking three or four extra stitches on the folds of the mitered corners to hold them in place.

About the Author

Jo Morton is a quiltmaker, fabric designer, teacher, author, and lecturer. Her use of color and design, as well as her fine stitchery, give her quilts the feeling of being made in the nineteenth century. Using an antique quilt as a source of inspiration, she creates an interpretation. Her quilts complement both country and contemporary settings, and her work is included in private and public collections across the country.

In 1980, Jo took her first quilting class, and in 1985 she created her first "made to look old" quilt. She determined early on that if she ever hoped to make all the quilts she wanted to make, they would have to be small, and this size works perfectly in the 1929 tiny bungalow where she lives.

Jo is well-known for her "Jo's Little Women Club" patterns, available through participating quilt shops since 2003. Her quilts have appeared in numerous magazines, and she's made several television appearances: HGTV's *Simply Quilts* episode 603; PBS's *Love of Quilting* episodes 1408 and 1805; and *The Quilt Show* episode 808, which airs on the internet via subscription.

Jo lives in Nebraska City with her husband, Russ, and two kitties, Socks and Chloe. Visit JoMortonQuilts.com to learn more. Follow Jo on Instagram at joquilts.

Acknowledgments

My thanks to the staff at Martingale. This book has let me revisit some of my favorite small quilts, and happily there are lots more for another day! The Martingale staff has been wonderful to work with. I was lucky to be part of the photography shoot for this book, which was fun and exhausting at the same time.

Thanks to Maggi Honeyman of Plano, Texas, who makes my quilts better with her beautiful quilting.

Many thanks to Mary Fornoff, Cindy Hansen, and Phyllis Masters for their piecing and pressing skills during Sewing Saturdays. I always look forward to our fun/work days together. These special friends have been helping me sew my quilts for the past 10 years.

To Ramona Collins, thanks for piecing "Indigo Stars Doll Quilt."

Sheri Dowding, my friend and former neighbor, thanks for being there to help where needed. Sheri hand stitches the bindings on my quilts, cuts fabric for me, helps at my retreats, and even "kittysits" for us. She's my ever-faithful friend and girl Friday.

My dear husband, Russ, thank you for doing whatever needs to be done. No matter the errand or chore, he is there.

A special acknowledgment to my mother, Mary E. Gress, who passed away in October 2014 at the age of 92. She always believed in and encouraged me. She taught me to do my best work on everything. I've sewn all my life, thanks to her. I'm blessed now to have her as an angel watching over me.

One other acknowledgment: The white mohair rabbit in the photo on page 21 was made by bear artist Lori Ann Corelis of Westerville, Ohio. It's one of the many treasures I have from the days of exhibiting at folk-art shows.